TRAFFICKING IN BROKEN HEARTS

Edwin Sánchez

D1600443

BROADWAY PLAY PUBLISHING INC
224 E 62nd St, NY NY 10065-8201
212 772-8334 fax: 212 772-8358
BroadwayPlayPubl.com

The play was first published by B P P I in February 1997 in the collection *Plays By Edwin Sánchez* First printing of this edition: December 2011 I S B N: 978-0-88145-498-7

Book design: Marie Donovan
Page make-up: Adobe Indesign
Typeface: Palatino
Printed and bound in the U S A

ABOUT THE AUTHOR

Recent productions include TRAFFICKING IN
BROKEN HEARTS at the Celebration Theater in Los
Angeles as well as the world premiere of his romantic
comedy I'LL TAKE ROMANCE at the Evolution
Theater Company in Ohio. His newest play LA BELLA
FAMILIA will be produced by Teatro Vista in Chicago
in 2011. Other productions include, DIOSA, produced
by Hartford Stage after a successful workshop by New
York Stage and Film, TRAFFICKING IN BROKEN
HEARTS at the Atlantic Theater Company in New
York, UNMERCIFUL GOOD FORTUNE at the Intar
Theater in New York, ICARUS produced by Fourth
Unity in New York, Actors Theater of Louisville as
part of their Humana Festival, and San Jose Rep in
California. His play BAREFOOT BOY WITH SHOES
ON was produced by Primary Stages in New York
and was selected by the Eugene O'Neill Playwrights
Conference to represent the National Playwrights
Conference at the Schelykovo Playwrights Seminar
in Russia. Mr Sánchez' work has been produced
regionally throughout the United States as well as
Brazil and Switzerland. Among his awards are the
Kennedy Center Fund for New American Plays
(CLEAN), three New York Foundation for the Arts
Playwriting/Screenwriting Fellowships, the Princess
Grace Playwriting Fellowship (UNMERCIFUL
GOOD FORTUNE), the Daryl Roth Creative Spirit

Award and the A T & T On Stage New Play Award
(UNMERCIFUL GOOD FORTUNE). Mr Sánchez lives
in upstate New York where he continues to write as
well as teach and mentor playwrights.

TRAFFICKING IN BROKEN HEARTS was first produced by Bailiwick Repertory, Chicago IL during the 1992 Pride Performance Series.

TRAFFICKING IN BROKEN HEARTS was subsequently produced in New York in 1994 by the Atlantic Theater Company (Neil Pepe, Artistic Director; Joshua Lehrer, Managing Director). The cast and creative contributors were:

PAPO .... Giancarlo Esposito
BRIAN .... Neil Pepe
BOBBY .... Anthony Rapp

Director .... Anna D Shapiro
Set & light design .... Kevin Rigdon
Costume design .... Laura Cunningham
Sound design .... One Dream Sound
Original music .... Max Shapiro
Fight choreography .... Rick Sordelet

CHARACTERS & SETTING

PAPO, *a hustler, 26 years old*
BRIAN, *a lawyer, 26 years old*
BOBBY, *a runaway, 16 years old*
Assorted voices that will represent the voices of New York

The play takes place primarily in the 42nd Street area of New York City.

(At rise: From the darkness neon begins to turn on and off. Voices are heard, some dirty talk, some high-pitched laughter. Drugs and sex are offered. All we see are flashing lights. The lights slowly come up to a dim. A fight is happening somewhere, a siren, someone asking for spare change while another voice is demanding that gentlemen drop their quarters. We see the facade of a peep show. PAPO, his back to the audience, stretches and yawns. He opens his pants and positions his cock to maximum advantage. He clears his throat and spits. He leans against the peep show facade. Lights begin to dim.)

PAPO: Hey, you wanna see a movie?

(Blackout)

(A third of the stage is lit.)

PAPO: The first time I walked down Forty-second Street I got scared and turned back. A woman lifted her skirt and started pissing and two cops were standing right there and they didn't do anything. She wasn't wearing panties and she was ugly. I turn around and walk back. I didn't go back for a while.

(Second third is lit. BRIAN at work. Sitting behind a desk he places a call. Music under.)

BRIAN: Hello.

VOICE 1: Card number, please.

(BRIAN fumbles in pocket for wallet. He removes a card.)

BRIAN: Uh, 0655182.

VOICE 1: Thank you. Go ahead.

BRIAN: Hello.

VOICE 2: Hi.

BRIAN: Hi.

VOICE 2: (*Pause)* You got a real sexy voice.

BRIAN: You too. Can you tell me what you look like?

VOICE 2: Sure. I'm six feet tall, a hundred-and-eighty, body builder, nine inches.

BRIAN: Sounds good.

VOICE 2: What are you in the mood for today?

BRIAN: I just want to hear your voice.

VOICE 2: You want me to talk dirty to you?

BRIAN: No, just talk to me.

VOICE 2: Look, what scene do you want?

(The music builds. Hard. Hypnotic. VOICE 2 fades and BRIAN will speak but won't be heard over the music. His phone receiver exchanges hands and his right hand goes under his desk. He opens his pants and begins to masturbate. The music becomes louder and he is sweating. He moans and trembles as he comes. A second after he does a light from an open doorway appears on him. He freezes. Music stops.)

SECRETARY'S VOICE: They're waiting for you in the conference room, Mister Ritter.

BRIAN: Tell them I'll be right in.

(Light from doorway disappears.)

VOICE 2: Are you still there? Hello.

(BRIAN hangs up. He pulls a handkerchief from his pocket and cleans himself.)

(Last third of the stage is lit. BOBBY is sitting on the floor, hugging himself and crying.)

BOBBY: Why do you want to marry her, Reggie? What's the matter with me? What's the matter with me?

(42nd Street peep show. PAPO is leaning against the front. Enter BRIAN from off stage. He slows down in front of peep show. He enters. PAPO waits a couple of seconds then follows. BRIAN is walking past the magazines. He stops to flip through one. PAPO reaches in front of him to get one.)

PAPO: 'Scuse me.

(BRIAN looks at PAPO out of the corner of his eye. PAPO brushes past him on the way to the booths. BRIAN waits a couple of seconds then fumbles, putting magazine back. BRIAN enters the booth area and pretends to read the display cards on the different booths.)

PAPO: Psst.

(BRIAN looks in the booth next to him where the door is ajar. PAPO is inside booth, playing with himself through his pants.)

PAPO: Hey man, you wanna see a movie?

(BRIAN stands, watching as PAPO begins to unfasten his pants.)

MAN'S VOICE: Let's drop some quarters, gentlemen.

(PAPO gestures with his head for BRIAN to come in. BRIAN is frozen in place.)

PAPO: C'mon man. I ain't giving no fucking free show.

BRIAN: The sign says one person per booth. What if they catch us?

PAPO: Nobody pays attention to that.

(BRIAN looks both ways and quickly enters the booth.)

PAPO: You got some quarters, man? You gotta drop some quarters in the machine else we can't close the door.

(BRIAN begins to look through his pockets.)

BRIAN: Yeah, I got a couple.

PAPO: Well, drop 'em in.

(BRIAN *does. The lights go out in the booth and a loop begins to play. They are standing in front of the screen so the film images are on their faces.* PAPO *leans against the wall, still massaging himself.*)

PAPO: Go ahead and touch it. It ain't gonna bite you.

(PAPO *reaches over and grabs one of* BRIAN's *hands. He places it over his crotch and moves it up and down.*)

PAPO: You got some money?

BRIAN: Uh-huh.

PAPO: Okay then.

(BRIAN *awkwardly grabs* PAPO *and tries to kiss him.* PAPO *pushes him off.*)

PAPO: Look man, I don't kiss no faggots.

BRIAN: Aren't you a faggot?

PAPO: No dickface, I'm a hustler. Look, you got some money, right?

BRIAN: Yeah.

PAPO: Okay, gimme twenty.

BRIAN: What for?

PAPO: To go down on me.

BRIAN: I don't know if I want to do that.

MAN'S VOICE: Let's drop some quarters, gentlemen.

(BRIAN *deposits another quarter.*)

PAPO: Not you. When the lights go up that's when you put in another quarter.

BRIAN: I'm sorry. Look, I've never done this before.

PAPO: Yeah, sure. It's still twenty. No discounts.

BRIAN: Can I kiss you?

PAPO: I told you, I don't kiss no faggots.

(BRIAN *shrugs helplessly and turns to leave.* PAPO *presses against him. He begins feeling him up, looking for his wallet.*)

PAPO: Hey c'mon, man. Relax.

BRIAN: Do you have someplace else we can go?

(PAPO *does not find a wallet in* BRIAN'*s pants.*)

PAPO: That would be more money.

BRIAN: That's okay.

PAPO: Man, you don't have any money. Don't be fucking bullshitting me.

(*Lights come up in booth.*)

BRIAN: Yes I do.

PAPO: Yeah? Show me.

(BRIAN *is about to reach for his money when a banging is heard on their booth door.*)

MAN'S VOICE: Let's drop some quarters in there.

PAPO: (*Under his breath*) Fuck you.

BRIAN: I don't have any more quarters.

PAPO: Great. (*He reaches into his pocket and pulls one out.*) You owe me a quarter, mother fucker. (*He deposits it.*) Let me go out first. I'll meet you outside then I'll take you to my room.

BRIAN: Okay.

PAPO: Hey man, you owe me a quarter.

(PAPO *exits.* BRIAN *touches the screen. Outside* PAPO *is waiting.* BRIAN *comes out of the peep show.*)

BRIAN: I got more change from a man in there. Here's your quarter.

PAPO: Yeah, look, it'll be fifty for me and ten dollars for the room.

BRIAN: I haven't got much time left.

PAPO: Don't worry, it won't take much time.

BRIAN: Maybe we should leave it for another time.

PAPO: You ain't got the money, right? Goddamn, fucking queer.

BRIAN: Please be quiet. No, I got it. It's right here. (*He takes his wallet from his jacket pocket but when he looks inside he only finds a ten.*) I'm sorry but all I have is a ten.

PAPO: Yeah, well you owe me that for the feel you copped in the booth.

BRIAN: Look, I got a credit card. I could buy you something.

PAPO: I don't want nothing. Fuck the credit card. What you gonna buy me?

BRIAN: I don't know. There's a clothing store over there, pick something.

PAPO: And you buy it for me?

(BRIAN *and* PAPO *approach store.*)

PAPO: How about that suit?

BRIAN: That's a hundred and twenty-five.

PAPO: Oh yeah.

BRIAN: How about that sweater?

PAPO: That's sixty-five.

BRIAN: It'll look good on you.

PAPO: So will the suit, man.

BRIAN: Wait here.

(BRIAN *enters shop. Lights fade. Up on flophouse.* BRIAN *and* PAPO *enter.* PAPO *is admiring his sweater.*)

BRIAN: Where's the washroom?

PAPO: This fucking sweater is ace.

BRIAN: Where can we clean up?

PAPO: Right there in the sink. They's supposed to give you a little soap and a towel but they won't if you don't ask for it.

BRIAN: Look.

PAPO: Papo.

BRIAN: Yeah, Papo. I have never done this before. With any man. Ever. I just want to be safe.

PAPO: Well, you shouldn't a bought me the sweater first, but it's okay. A lot of guys would have gotten the sweater and skipped but not me. I'll treat you right.

BRIAN: I don't want to get a disease.

PAPO: Excuse me?

BRIAN: I don't know where you've been and I know that's none of my business; but I don't want to die—

PAPO: Hey man, you think I got AIDS?

BRIAN: I'm not saying you do. I'm just saying—

PAPO: I ain't no fucking leper.

BRIAN: I've waited this long I can wait until they find a cure.

PAPO: So fucking wait.

BRIAN: Are you healthy?

PAPO: Jesus Christ, you wanna fucking note from my mother?

BRIAN: I'm afraid.

PAPO: Well look, what the fuck do you want me to do?

BRIAN: I'm afraid.

PAPO: Look, what do you want to do? Do you wanna jerk off?

BRIAN: I don't have to buy you a sweater so I can jerk myself off.

PAPO: Lissen, I ain't got all day and you ain't got all day; so what is it you want?

BRIAN: Just be a little patient. I've never done this before.

PAPO: Yeah yeah, sure sure.

BRIAN: Please don't ruin it for me.

PAPO: What the fuck am I doing? You're the one looking at me like an open sore or something.

BRIAN: I'm afraid to touch you. I'm becoming so obsessed with sex that I'm suffocating. I walk down Forty-second Street and I can't breathe.

PAPO: You ain't missing much.

BRIAN: I'm beginning to fantasize at work.

PAPO: Hey, fucking ease up. Look, I'm clean. You ain't gonna catch nothing from me. I use these. (*He throws a package of condoms on the bed.*)

BRIAN: Great.

PAPO: Let's get this show on the road. I'll pop your cherry and you'll feel like a new man.

(PAPO *carefully takes off his sweater and folds it neatly.* BRIAN *picks up the package of condoms.*)

BRIAN: I am trusting my life to a piece of rubber that is thin enough to read through.

PAPO: C'mon, mother fucker. They're tropical colors no less.

BRIAN: I can't. I want to, but I can't.

(PAPO *stares at* BRIAN.)

PAPO: Fine. Fuck you, too. But I am keeping this sweater.

BRIAN: Don't be mad.

PAPO: Hey, of course not. But lissen, I better not see you on the deuce again `cause sweater or no sweater I'll kick your mother-fucking ass in.

BRIAN: Don't be that way.

PAPO: Come telling me I'm a fucking walking den of AIDS. What, you work for the *Post*, mother fucker?

BRIAN: Papo, can I just hold you.

PAPO: No.

BRIAN: I just want to feel you next to me.

PAPO: (*Relenting*) Fuck you.

(BRIAN *tentatively approaches* PAPO. PAPO *smirks, but lets himself be hugged.*)

PAPO: Shit, it was an expensive sweater.

(BRIAN *begins to caress* PAPO, *who slowly begins to respond.*)

PAPO: Look, mother fucker—

BRIAN: Brian.

PAPO: Brian. You ain't gonna catch that shit from me. I'm clean. Really. No tracks. Look at my arms.

BRIAN: Just hold me.

PAPO: You a virgin, right? I never met a fucking virgin before.

BRIAN: If I'm fucking I can't be a virgin.

PAPO: You know what I fucking mean.

(PAPO *and* BRIAN *begin to kiss.* PAPO *begins to undress* BRIAN, *who panics and tries to break free.* PAPO *holds him.*

BRIAN *pushes him, breaks free, and runs out.* PAPO *follows him. On the street.)*

PAPO: C'mon back, man. You still got some time left.

BRIAN: You weren't supposed to do that.

PAPO: Okay. Okay.

BRIAN: I know where you were heading.

PAPO: Jesus fucking Christ. I'm sorry I touched you. I thought that's what you paid me for.

BRIAN: Lower your voice.

PAPO: Look, you turn me on. Not many tricks do that. I gotta fake it with most of 'em. But you, look. (*He points to his crotch.)* I don't wear underwears so I know when something is fucking getting to me.

(BRIAN *is panic stricken. He walks away from* PAPO *and pretends to look in a store window.* PAPO *follows him.)*

PAPO: What's the matter?

BRIAN: Will you cover that?

PAPO: C'mon. Nobody gives a fuck.

(BRIAN *walks away,* PAPO *follows.)*

PAPO: Man, you don't want to see it, you don't want to touch it. Get yourself a fucking woman.

(BRIAN *tries to stretch* PAPO's *sweater down to cover his crotch.)*

PAPO: Hey, watch it with the fucking sweater.

BRIAN: Uh, look, I thought it was the right time for me but I guess it's not.

PAPO: Hey c'mon. There's no mother-fucking contest going on. We ain't out to break a speed limit or shit like that.

BRIAN: Papo, I am a twenty-six-year-old virgin.

PAPO: You're twenty-six? You look older.

BRIAN: There are not too many of us out there.

PAPO: It's probably `cause of the fucking suit and tie.

BRIAN: Look, I've got to go.

PAPO: You wanna meet again or something?

BRIAN: I'm...I'm not ready.

PAPO: Give you a discount. I could use some pants to go with this sweater.

BRIAN: And buy yourself some underwear. People are staring at us.

PAPO: Fuck 'em. You wanna get back together again?

BRIAN: I have to get back to work.

PAPO: Hey, I'm not good enough for you, faggot.

(BRIAN *walks away.* PAPO *follows.*)

PAPO: Look, I'm sorry. I'm sorry. My mouth is like on automatic pilot.

(BRIAN *grabs* PAPO's *hand and shakes it.*)

BRIAN: Goodbye and good luck.

(BRIAN *hurriedly crosses the street.*)

PAPO: Yeah, you too.

(PAPO *waits for a bit and then follows* BRIAN *to where he works.* BRIAN *rushes into the building not knowing he has been followed.* PAPO *smiles at the building.*)

(*Lights up on* BOBBY, *who is packing a knapsack full of panties.*)

BOBBY: Dear Reggie, thanks a lot for telling me yourself that you were gonna get married. It meant a whole lot to me that you called even though Mom and Dad were trying to keep it a secret. We both know how they are. Reggie, I think you are making a big mistake. There is

no way this Lisa can love you the way I love you and
no way you can love her the way you love your Baby.
I'm going to save you, Reggie, before you make the
worst mistake of our lives. Love, Baby.

(Lights up on PAPO *sitting at a table, drinking coffee.)*

PAPO: I always take a coffee at Blimpie's on Forty-
second off Eighth. Right across the street from Port
Authority. Pick up some change from the Jersey crowd.
I used to hang out at Playland next to the old Anco
Theatre, but fuck, the crowd there just kept getting
younger and younger. Fucking Menudo convention.
One of those snot-nosed little bastards tried to charge
me. Waving his skinny ass in my face and then tells me
"forty bucks". I broke his head. They don't want me at
Playland no more. Fuck 'em. I don't care. I'm here for
the duration.

(Lights come up on BOBBY, *who is holding a carving knife.*
PAPO *remains lit, drinking his coffee silently.)*

BOBBY: No, not a whole set of knives. I think all my
sister-in-law needs is a carving knife. The whole family
is getting together for her birthday and I'm always
giving her clothes and stuff so I figured this year I'd
give her something for the house. She likes cooking
so I'm sure she'll be able to utilize it. My sister-in-law
really is gonna be surprised. I think mine is gonna be
the best gift of all.

(Lights out on BOBBY.)

PAPO: And anyways right outside of Playland there's
this girl preaching to everybody with a mother-fuckin'
bullhorn. Yeah, that bitch. Goddamn. It's like, is Jesus
Christ deaf?

(Lights up on BRIAN. *He is at his desk, lost in thought. The
phone on his desk rings seven times without any sign of*

BRIAN *hearing it. After the phone has stopped ringing there is a pause,* BRIAN *suddenly talks into the intercom.)*

BRIAN: Did the phone just ring?

PAPO: After I recharge my batteries at Blimpie's I head to P A. You gotta be careful though `cause they put mother-fucking cops everywhere. Keep moving and keep looking at the schedule so it looks like you got someplace to go. I once got pinched after I sucked a cop dry. Hell, yes! He starts in to read me my mother-fucking rights and I looked at that mother fucker and I started yelling "Rape" and he got nervous and he left.

(Lights up. PAPO *and* BOBBY *meet—the men's room at the Port Authority, five P M on Friday.* BOBBY *looks like what he is, lost. He is wearing a jacket that is too hot for the weather and carrying a knapsack. In his right hand he carries the knife in a brown paper bag. He is hot and tired. He squats down on the floor and puts his knapsack between his legs and the paper bag on top of it. He is removing his jacket when* PAPO *enters and walks right into him.)*

PAPO: Hey mother fucker, you couldn't find someplace else to park?

BOBBY: You bumped into me.

*(*PAPO *does not listen and continues walking.)*

BOBBY: You did.

*(*PAPO *has walked down the length of the stalls and returns. He is upset. Again he bumps into* BOBBY.*)*

PAPO: Goddamn it, kid. Get the fuck outta my way.

BOBBY: You bumped into me.

PAPO: What?

BOBBY: Last time too.

*(*PAPO *grabs* BOBBY'*s face.)*

PAPO: If I see you again I'm gonna kick your fuckin' ass in.

(*Someone clears his throat in the last stall.* PAPO *releases* BOBBY *and washes his hands.*)

VOICE: Psst.

BOBBY: What's that?

PAPO: Why don't you go over there and find out, cunt?

VOICE: Psst, hey kid.

PAPO: He means you, white boy.

BOBBY: He dropped some money.

PAPO: No, fool, he's makin' an offer you ain't gonna refuse.

BOBBY: I'm hungry.

PAPO: Tell him that. Maybe the mother fucker will buy you dinner.

BOBBY: I spent all my money on a gift.

VOICE: Psst.

BOBBY: You wanna see?

PAPO: Show it to the guy with the leak.

BOBBY: What do I have to do for the money?

PAPO: Nothing you haven't done before, only now some fool mother fucker's gonna pay to help.

BOBBY: I could use the money.

PAPO: So go ahead.

BOBBY: Can I?

PAPO: Hey faggot, I ain't your father.

(BOBBY *begins to inch toward the stall.*)

BOBBY: I'm sorry I bumped into you.

(PAPO *watches* BOBBY's *slow progress in the mirror.*)

PAPO: Oh, what the hell.

(PAPO *grabs* BOBBY's *arm and steers him out of the men's room.*)

PAPO: Come on, Georgie, we don't want you to miss your mother-fucking bus. You know how ma gets.

BOBBY: Bobby.

PAPO: Yeah, just move it, white boy.

(*Outside of the men's room*)

PAPO: Let's circulate. That guy in the last stall. The one you was going to is a cop. The second you touched that twenty he was gonna pinch your lily-white ass.

BOBBY: Why would a cop wanna pinch me?

PAPO: Arrest, fool. Fuck. Straight off the mother fuckin' bus. He'd have you for soliciting and as a runaway.

BOBBY: How do you know he's a cop?

PAPO: They all wear the same fucking shoes. All the time. Like the whole fucking police force gets a discount if they all buy them. Ugly-ass shoes.

BOBBY: I'm still hungry.

PAPO: So, go earn some money, bitch. Just watch out for the shoes.

(BOBBY *takes out a cigarette, lights it, and begins to smoke.* PAPO *immediately takes the cigarette from his mouth, throws it on the floor, and steps on it.*)

PAPO: Babies don't smoke.

(PAPO *walks away;* BOBBY *follows.*)

PAPO: Goodbye, Kid.

BOBBY: I'll give you my jacket if I can stay with you for a while.

PAPO: I don't want your fucking jacket.

BOBBY: I want ice cream.

PAPO: Bitch, what is your problem. Lookee here. (*He goes to trash basket and takes out a piece of paper.*) Pencil.

BOBBY: I got a pen.

PAPO: Whatever.

(BOBBY *reaches into his pocket and gives* PAPO *a pen.* PAPO *looks at the arrival board and writes down a number.*)

PAPO: Okay, Kid, every time you walk up to somebody you tell him this is the bus you're waiting for. He'll tell you it ain't due for hours you tell him you're waiting for your mother and you haven't got any money and you're hungry. With a face like yours, Baby, they'll buy you something. Don't go with one of them unless they show you money. First get the money then find out what you gotta do to earn it. *Capiche?* Keep your eyes on their shoes, too. If a cop stops you show him this piece of paper and point to the fucking sign. Then just tell him you're gonna sit down and read comic books. They should leave you the fuck alone.

BOBBY: Who am I waiting for again?

PAPO: Your mother, asshole.

BOBBY: Right. You want to wait with me?

PAPO: You are a fool. This is just pretend so the cops don't get you. Gimme back the paper. You're gonna fuck it up.

BOBBY: I won't. Honest.

PAPO: Shit. I should just let them drag you down to juvenile. Trade down there rape you ragged.

(BOBBY *begins to tremble. He drops his bag.*)

PAPO: Hey shithead, don't go having a fucking seizure on me. You a fucking epileptic or something?

BOBBY: I'm just hungry, Reggie. Buy me some ice cream.

PAPO: Sure, Baby, sure. They got some Howard Johnson shit on the second floor.

BOBBY: My mother's not coming to pick me up. Can I stay with you?

PAPO: What the fuck. I ain't scored and I'm horny and you're cute. Okay. One night. One. Uno.

(BOBBY *picks up his bag. Blackout. Light up on* BRIAN *in a cap and gown, holding a diploma. It is his graduation day.*)

DEAN'S VOICE: ...class valedictorian, Brian Ritter.

BRIAN: Esteemed professors, honored guests, fellow students—

(BRIAN'*s taped voice will continue but his mouth will stop moving.*)

BRIAN'S VOICE: We have before us what appears to be a horizon with no borders, no limits. Our education and our potential guarantee us entrance to—

BRIAN: To nothing. My tie is too tight. I remember I was angry because the gown wasn't long enough to hide where my mother had lowered the hem of my cousin David's "perfectly good suit, and we can't afford a new one anyway." I am the class valedictorian in a hand-me-down suit. Voted most desperate to fit in. I always knew I was different and I always hid it. Ever since my parents caught me playing doctor with a neighbor boy. They wouldn't speak to me for a week. I was dirty. I didn't exist. Sometimes I would get so crazy I would kiss my G I Joe doll. Or I would cry and stand in a corner, praying that God would make it all better. That I would be like everybody else. What kind of parents wouldn't talk to a seven-year-old child for a week? I am getting out of here. I will become a somebody. I will win my independence. I will buy my life back from you. And when I have I'll get myself a man. A life-sized G I Joe. If I can just wait. If I can go hungry just for a little while I'll be all right.

BRIAN'S VOICE: ...and in closing—

BRIAN: There's no reason anyone should know. Don't make the world angry at you, Brian. Wait.

BRIAN'S VOICE: Wait.

BRIAN: Wait.

BRIAN'S VOICE: Thank you.

(*Blackout. Lights up on flophouse.*)

BOBBY: Why can't I stay with you? I'll sleep on the floor. You won't even know I'm here.

PAPO: That's `cause you won't be. Go get your own room, though you'll probably get kilt by some doped-up jerk. Go home, Kid.

BOBBY: Why don't you want me?

PAPO: Oh shit, c'mon, Kid, if you're gonna start getting all pussy on me.

BOBBY: You saved my life.

PAPO: I shoulda let the cop throw you into juvenile hall.

BOBBY: They'd kill me in there.

PAPO: Man, all those Puerto Ricans and Blacks get together and they'd rip your fucking ass in half.

BOBBY: My two older brothers would rape me `cause I was so beautiful. Ever since I was twelve. One would hold me down and the other would rape me.

PAPO: Yeah, life's a bitch.

BOBBY: They took Polaroid pictures. They would wait until my parents were gone and make me put on my mother's clothes.

PAPO: Real Norman Rockwell stuff, white boy.

BOBBY: My parents divorced when they found the pictures. Why did they do that? They sent my brothers away to a military school and me to a nut house. My father got married again. He has a little girl, a real one. Doesn't ever want me to come over. My mother puts a lock on her closet door when I'm home with her.

PAPO: Sure, stupid. She's afraid you're gonna steal her clothes.

BOBBY: I wouldn't do that.

PAPO: I was just goofing on you, Kid.

BOBBY: My brother's getting married. That's where I was supposed to be going when I got off the bus. He found somebody else. He used to call me his Baby.

PAPO: You is all a bunch of sick fucks.

BOBBY: Reggie always treated me nice. He got me a valentine once.

PAPO: I didn't know they made them for brothers. Lissen, you're a cute kid. You'll find yourself a nice rich guy who'll take care of you. You're a fine piece of blue-eyed ass, you'll do okay.

BOBBY: I want to be your wife.

PAPO: What, do I look like your brother? Is there a blue-eyed blond football player in me that I'm not seeing? Man, last night was just a freebie, don't let it go to your head. This is just too fucking stupid for words.

BOBBY: I can cook.

PAPO: Great, so can Burger King.

BOBBY: You can pimp me. You said yourself that I was a fine piece of ass. We can make a lot of money.

PAPO: I can make a lot of money.

BOBBY: Right, you can make a lot of money.

PAPO: No, forget it. That's all I need, for the fucking cops that's got it in for me already to see me pimping a little white minor.

BOBBY: I'm not a minor.

PAPO: Save it, Baby.

BOBBY: I can steal for you. (*He pulls a small radio out of his pocket.*) Look, I took this from the guy sitting next to me on the bus. For you.

PAPO: Yeah?

BOBBY: I took it right out of his pocket. I could make you a lot of money, between stealing and making tricks.

PAPO: That's turning tricks, man. You stole this? Then how come it has your name in magic marker on the back?

BOBBY: I wrote it.

PAPO: Yeah? Bullshit. Let me see the marker you used.

BOBBY: I threw it away. It was evidence.

PAPO: Right. You can't steal and you're gonna make a fucking great hustler proposing to every john you get.

BOBBY: I'm sorry, Sir.

PAPO: Don't call me Sir. I ain't your fucking father, Baby.

BOBBY: I didn't lie about cooking. I know how to cook.

PAPO: Then fucking go get yourself a job at some dago place. Go to a Greek diner and slice up some gyros.

(PAPO *turns to leave.* BOBBY *pulls the knife from his jacket. He stabs at* PAPO, *barely missing him.*)

PAPO: You fucking crazy?!

BOBBY: Why can't I stay with you? (*He jumps in front of the door.*)

PAPO: I don't want to have to hurt you, Kid. Don't be pulling no knives on me.

BOBBY: Call me "Baby".

(PAPO *tries to push* BOBBY, *who stabs wildly at him. He slashes* PAPO's *sweater sleeve.* PAPO *falls backwards on the floor.* BOBBY *holds the knife, poised at* PAPO's *throat.*)

BOBBY: Please call me "Baby".

PAPO: Baby.

BOBBY: I was going to Reggie's wedding. I was. I was going to stop his marriage to that imposter. It's a good thing I met you. Now I can be yours.

PAPO: Yeah, Baby. Whatever you say.

BOBBY: You're just like Reggie was, too. You can be real rough in bed but every so often you'd kiss as if you hoped I wouldn't notice. You'd kiss my eyelids. So softly. Give me a kiss, Sir.

(BOBBY *and* PAPO *kiss with the knife still at* PAPO's *throat.*)

BOBBY: I wanna do what we did last night. Whatever you want me to do. Can I call you Reggie?

PAPO: Sure.

BOBBY: And you can call me Baby. I'll make you a good wife.

(BOBBY *helps* PAPO *stand.*)

BOBBY: Take off your sweater, Reggie.

PAPO: My what?

BOBBY: Your sweater, Reggie.

(PAPO *slowly does.*)

BOBBY: I didn't hurt you, did I?

PAPO: No, it's okay. (*Pause*) Baby.

(BOBBY *groans.* PAPO *grabs* BOBBY *by the back of his hair and pulls him toward him, kissing him roughly on the mouth and then very gently on the eyelids.* BOBBY *is still holding the knife.* PAPO *continues to kiss him now on the neck and shoulders.* PAPO *kisses* BOBBY's *right arm, his hand, and then kisses the blade of the knife.*)

PAPO: Give me the knife, Baby.

(BOBBY *gives* PAPO *the knife.*)

PAPO: Lay down.

(BOBBY *does. His arms reach up for* PAPO. *Blackout. Lights up outside of Peep Show.* PAPO *is hanging out as* BRIAN *comes down the street. He sees* PAPO *and tries to walk quickly by.* PAPO *sees him and chases him.*)

PAPO: Hey Brian. Brian, wait up. (*He falls in step next to him.*) Hey man, you deaf or something?

BRIAN: I thought you people never recognize customers on the street.

PAPO: Well, fuck you very much, too.

BRIAN: I'm sorry. How are you doing?

PAPO: Okay. How about you?

BRIAN: Fine. Look, I've got to run.

PAPO: Run my ass. This is your lunch break. The only place you gotta run is to a peep show.

BRIAN: Papo.

PAPO: Which is cool `cause that's where I met you.

BRIAN: Hey, you need a couple of bucks?

PAPO: Shit, can't I talk to you without your wallet getting all itchy?

BRIAN: Sorry. What do you want?

PAPO: Well man, I see you're in the market for some action.

BRIAN: Papo.

PAPO: No strings.

BRIAN: I was kind of looking for somebody else.

PAPO: Yeah, well, fuck you.

(BRIAN *walks away.* PAPO *follows.*)

PAPO: Hey look man, I'm sorry. I haven't seen you in a while. I guess I'm jumpy, that's all. Friends?

BRIAN: Sure.

(PAPO *and* BRIAN *shake hands.*)

BRIAN: Look, I don't have much time left.

PAPO: We can just duck in here. I got some quarters.

BRIAN: How about your place?

PAPO: Uh, no. A friend is kinda staying there. A real sweet kid, a little psycho is all.

BRIAN: Why are you letting him stay?

PAPO: I don't know.

BRIAN: Is he your lover?

PAPO: Get real. Baby spends all day in panties.

BRIAN: Baby?

PAPO: The kid. The kid, okay. Hey, you jealous or something?

BRIAN: No.

PAPO: Yes you are. I sleep with this guy every night and he lets me do anything I want to him. You are jealous.

BRIAN: Papo, I really don't care.

PAPO: Yeah, I know you don't.

BRIAN: I should start getting back. I left a lot of work on my desk.

PAPO: Hey, a quickie. My treat.

BRIAN: Some other time.

PAPO: Let me walk you back then.

(BRIAN *stops* PAPO.)

BRIAN: No.

(PAPO *pushes* BRIAN's *hand away.*)

PAPO: Man, I just wanna be your friend. You think you're too good for me? Fine. Fuck you. I got me a piece of sixteen-year-old white meat who'll take anything I give him. Baby treats me just fine; so fuck you. Fuck you, mother fucker.

(BRIAN *hurries off with* PAPO *still screaming after him.*)

PAPO: Yeah, you're too good to talk to me but you ain't too good to get my dick up your ass. Fuck you, man, just fuck you. Look, how about if I call you sometime?

(*Blackout. Lights up as each person speaks.*)

BRIAN: It's crazy, but I know he follows me. He thinks I don't notice, but I do. What does he want from me? He can't be in love. People like that don't fall in love and nobody falls in love with me. So what does he want?

BOBBY: I'm making him everything I ever wanted in a brother.

PAPO: (*Holding a brick*) This is where I grew up. This brick belongs to a building in the Bronx. Six-story walk-up. Fucking got asthma from living there. Going up and down those mother-fucking stairs every day. I went there a couple of years ago and the fucking building was bricked up. I hadn't been there in ten years and I expect to go back and knock on the door, tell the new people I had lived there and if I could have a fucking look around. So I go back an' it's all like fucking bricked up and I thought I should have gone back sooner.

BRIAN: Am I supposed to be the "gateway to the white world" for him?

BOBBY: And he loves me, too.

PAPO: I went back last summer and the whole place was torn down. That's when I got the brick. Sure you can tear a building down but you can't knock it down from here. (*He points to heart with brick.*)

PAPO: People don't fucking understand that. My parents live in P R now. I send them money, they don't ask questions. My baby sister lives with them. She's getting married soon.

BOBBY: I would like for us to get married. To be together for always so no one can separate us.

BRIAN: The thing is Papo doesn't know about the times I follow him. When I stand there without him seeing me and just watch him. He doesn't know the times he's helped me jerk off.

BOBBY: Don't tell Papo but I went upstate the other day. I wanted to see Reggie. I wanted to tell him it was all right. That I forgave him for getting married cause I was gonna get married, too. I'm on the bus and just as we enter into town I see Reggie outside of his car. I get off and run to him. Ronald, my other brother, was with him.

PAPO: Baby's like a pet, you know.

BOBBY: They wanted to take me back to the hospital. They say I'm sick. They say what we did together was sick and Reggie can't meet my eyes. Ronald's doing all the talking. And I tell them I got a good man, a true man. Someone who really loves me.

BRIAN: Maybe if Papo and I ran away together.

BOBBY: Ronald grabs me and I kick him in the balls. He's down. He yells for Reggie to hold me and when he does I naturally kiss him. Like always. And he looks at me and yells, "Run!" He sets me free and holds back Ronald and I hitched a ride with a trucker to the Lincoln Tunnel. I'm luckier than they are. I get to go home to someone who loves me.

(*Blackout. Lights up.* PAPO *is in the receptionist area of* BRIAN's *office.*)

RECEPTIONIST: Pick-up or delivery?

PAPO: No, I'm here to see Brian.

RECEPTIONIST: Do you have an appointment with Mister Ritter?

PAPO: Nah, it's a surprise. Just tell him Papo is here. Uh, Mister Papo Santiago. (*He can feel people looking at him. He tries to act nonchalant but finally smirks at a few people. He takes a paper cup and gets water from a water cooler. He is nervous and fidgets with the glass, accidentally puncturing it and spilling the water.*) Oh shit, I'm sorry. You got a rag or something? These little glasses are for shit.

(BRIAN *enters. He tries to hide his anger as he steers* PAPO *outside. He pushes him into a stairwell.*)

PAPO: Hey man, what's with you? No hello—

BRIAN: Don't you ever—

PAPO: —no nothing. Just take me off to—

BRIAN: —ever come to where I work again.

PAPO: Huh?

BRIAN: How did you find it? Did you follow me?

PAPO: Wait a second. Are you pissed off that I came to visit?

BRIAN: This is not a place for you to visit. This is where I work.

PAPO: Big fucking deal.

BRIAN: I'm serious. You are never to come—

PAPO: Fuck off, man. I just wanted to surprise you.

BRIAN: —here again. What the hell were you thinking of? Look at the way you look.

PAPO: What the hell's the matter with the way I look?

BRIAN: You look like a goddamn faggot.

(PAPO *punches* BRIAN.)

PAPO: Look, mother fucker, I come by `cause I was gonna take you to lunch.

BRIAN: Dressed like that?

PAPO: Fuck you fuck you fuck you.

(BRIAN *tries to cover* PAPO's *mouth, who pushes his hand away.* BRIAN *tries to regain his composure.*)

BRIAN: Papo...I can't receive any visitors where I work. This is not playtime, this is work.

PAPO: I fucking know that, I'm not stupid. And don't be telling me you (*He hits* BRIAN.) can't get any visitors `cause everybody knows—

BRIAN: Will you just get out?

PAPO: —that you people all got your private little bars in your office for your guests. I seen that on the T V.

(BRIAN *reaches into his pocket and takes out his wallet. He gives* PAPO *some money.*)

BRIAN: Go buy something.

(PAPO *tries to jam the wallet into* BRIAN's *mouth.*)

PAPO: Look you piece of shit I ain't no piece of shit. (*He takes the money and wipes his ass with it.*) This is what I think of your money.

BRIAN: I'm sorry. I'm sorry. Please keep your voice down.

PAPO: I went out and bought underwears, okay? Something I ain't never done for anybody.

BRIAN: Okay, okay.

PAPO: No, it's not okay. I'm sorry you're embarrassed by me, faggot.

BRIAN: Please, get out of here.

(PAPO *pushes* BRIAN *against the wall. He pulls an open package of underwear from his jacket. There are still two left in the package. He throws them at* BRIAN.)

PAPO: Here, these are yours, mother fucker.

(PAPO *storms out.* BRIAN *picks up his wallet, the money, and the underwear. He removes one of the briefs from the jacket and kisses it.*)

(*The following scene is done with lights and sound.* PAPO *is standing between two subway cars on an express train. As the lights and the sound build so do his screams. He opens his pants and struggles until he manages to rip off his underwear. Lights fade. Train sounds fade.*)

(*Lights up on* BRIAN *in his bedroom. He is undressing. He removes* PAPO's *underwear from his pocket and puts a pair on. He fondles himself. He adjusts his mirror on the bureau so it can reflect on him. He lays on the bed and caresses himself, pinching his nipples.*)

BRIAN: Oh, Baby. You know that I want you so much. And you want it too, yes you do. You drive me crazy. I want to kiss every inch of your body.

(*Music begins underneath.*)

BRIAN: I've been watching you for so long. Now it's just you and me. All I want is to touch you and hold you. (*He runs his hands over his body. His eyes are shut tight.*) Oh, yes, and kiss you. (*He takes a pillow and begins to kiss it. He places another pillow between his legs.*) Nobody can see us. It's you and me, all alone. Don't we look good together? Look in the mirror. Don't we look good?

(BRIAN *opens his eyes.* PAPO's *voice is heard.*)

PAPO'S VOICE: You wanna see a movie?

(BRIAN *sits bolt upright. He looks straight into the mirror.*)

BRIAN: I've got to get out. I've got to get out. (*He reaches madly for the phone and dials.*)

VOICE: Hello, card number please.

BRIAN: Yes, 0655182.

VOICE: Thank you. Please hold.

MAN'S VOICE: Hi.

BRIAN: I want to touch you.

MAN'S VOICE: Yeah.

BRIAN: I want you right here.

PAPO'S VOICE: You turn me on. Not many tricks do that.

BRIAN: I gotta get out. I gotta get out of here. (*He jumps from the bed and throws on a pair of slacks and a jacket. He hurriedly puts on some shoes and runs to the door. He stands frozen in place in the open doorway, unable to set foot outside of his apartment.*) I can't, Papo. Please, I can't.

PAPO'S VOICE: I sleep with this guy every night. He lets me do anything I want to him.

(BRIAN *screams out into the hallway.*)

BRIAN: Papo! (*He slams the door and collapses against it.*)

(*Blackout. Lights up on flophouse.* BOBBY *is wearing panties and panties are hung to dry from every available place. Enter* PAPO, *who is still upset over his turndown at* BRIAN's *office.* BOBBY *senses trouble and tries to keep his distance.* PAPO *paces and begins to pull down the panties.*)

PAPO: I come home to a fucking laundromat.

BOBBY: I gotta put it somewhere to dry.

PAPO: They got dryers. God invented dryers, okay?

(BOBBY *is on his hands and knees picking up the panties.)*

BOBBY: I wash these at home, Darling. All my fine washables are done by hand.

PAPO: These are not yours. They belong to a woman. You know, a woman.

(PAPO *roughly grabs* BOBBY *and makes him stand. He grabs* BOBBY'*s balls.)*

PAPO: You're supposed to be a fucking guy.

(PAPO *pushes him aside.)*

BOBBY: I can be who I want to be, I can create myself. What's the matter, Reggie?

PAPO: Don't fucking call me Reggie! I'm confused enough as it is.

BOBBY: Are you hungry? Did you have a tough football practice? Why won't you tell Baby what's wrong?

(PAPO *grabs* BOBBY.)

PAPO: You ain't my Baby. I am not your goddamn fucking brother, see. Goddamn loony tunes. I want you out of here. You take your underwear and you make tracks back to the white world but you leave me the fuck alone.

MAN'S VOICE: Hey, you faggots wanna keep it down in there?

BOBBY: What would you do without me? You can't cook.

(PAPO *sits on the bed with his head in his hands.)*

PAPO: Leave me alone, man. Just leave me alone.

(BOBBY *kneels next to him.)*

BOBBY: I'm not a man, I'm your Baby.

(PAPO *puts his arm around* BOBBY's *shoulder and begins to rock him.*)

BOBBY: You just wait. Someday we'll get our own house, and a sheepdog, and two children.

PAPO: Fucking loony tunes.

BOBBY: And a station wagon. I'll drive you to the train station and you can catch the eight-fifteen into the city. I'll go home and get the kids off to school and clean the house and go shopping and make dinner. You know, I can really cook. (*He gets up and goes to hot plate. He returns with a pot.*) Look, I made Rice-a-roni. Your favorite, Reggie.

(PAPO *begins to tremble. He knocks the pot from* BOBBY's *hand and begins to beat him.*)

PAPO: I am not Reggie! You got that you little mother fucker? You are getting out of this place today, right now.

(BOBBY *is trying to block his blows.*)

BOBBY: Please, Reggie, please don't hit me. I'll do whatever you want.

PAPO: Goddamn fucking retard. (*He points to himself.*) Papo! You got that? (*He smacks him for emphasis.*) Papo!

(*He throws open the door and begins to throw* BOBBY's *panties into the hallway.* BOBBY *is crying and hanging on to* PAPO's *leg.*)

BOBBY: Please, Papo, please don't.

(*Steps are heard outside the door.*)

MAN'S VOICE: Hey, you wanna beat the little queer up? Fine. Just keep it down.

PAPO: This little mother fucker is outta here.

(BOBBY *is still crying and wrapped around* PAPO's *leg.*)

BOBBY: Why don't you want me, Reggie? Why? I wore the panties you wanted.

PAPO: I bought underwears!

BOBBY: You should have married me.

MAN'S VOICE: I personally don't care. I just don't want no trouble.

(PAPO *tries to move his leg but* BOBBY *holds on fast.*)

PAPO: It's okay, Baby.

BOBBY: Why didn't you tell me you didn't like Rice-a-roni?

MAN'S VOICE: Are you working this kid? Cute kid, you know?

PAPO: Hey man, throw me those mother fucking panties. (*He catches them. He gently rubs* BOBBY's *head with them.*)

BOBBY: Are you mad at me, Reggie?

PAPO: No, Baby, I'm not mad.

BOBBY: I'll do whatever you want me to do, you know that.

PAPO: Yeah, Baby, I know that.

(BOBBY *slowly stands and huddles under* PAPO's *arm.*)

MAN'S VOICE: Hey look, Papo, how much for the kid?

PAPO: Baby's not for sale.

MAN'S VOICE: C'mon guy.

PAPO: But you can watch.

BOBBY: Reggie.

PAPO: Sssh.

MAN'S VOICE: How much?

PAPO: Today's rent.

MAN'S VOICE: Forget it.

PAPO: Goodnight then, mother fucker.

MAN'S VOICE: And I can watch.

PAPO: That's what I said.

MAN'S VOICE: Okay.

BOBBY: No, Reggie.

PAPO: Look, Baby, what was the name of your other fucking brother?

BOBBY: Ronald.

(PAPO *pushes* BOBBY *backwards on the bed. Lights go out on bed. The only light is now coming from the doorway. Fade to blackout.* BRIAN *is leaning against his desk, coffee cup in hand. He speaks to a co-worker.*)

BRIAN: I'm sorry, my mind wandered, you were saying. No, it's just personal stuff. Someone I was seeing. We're both a little too career oriented if you know what I mean. No, you couldn't possibly. I do have a life outside of this office. Just `cause I don't spend Monday morning giving everybody a blow-by-blow account of my weekend doesn't mean I don't go out and...do stuff. Yeah, I've met somebody, but...it's over. I sort of blew my top. What I would really like to do is go away, the two of us, for a weekend maybe. Where we don't know anybody, and nobody knows us. Get to know each other a little more. Get to know each other, period. I don't know, maybe we could... there's no future in this. I want a future. I want what you have.

(BOBBY *is taping pictures from magazines on the wall. They are all bright and colorful.*)

PAPO: What you doing?

BOBBY: They're pretty, right?

(PAPO *shrugs.*)

PAPO: Where do you get the magazines?

BOBBY: From the trash.

PAPO: You don't have to be pulling no magazines from no trash. People don't have to see you like going through the fucking garbage. How do you think that makes me look.

BOBBY: Nobody saw me.

PAPO: Where do you get the tape?

(PAPO, *from his seated position, begins to jab his foot playfully into* BOBBY, *who continues his taping of pictures.*)

BOBBY: I took some money from your pocket.

(PAPO, *still playfully, jabs him a little harder.*)

PAPO: You don't even know enough to say you fucking borrowed it.

(BOBBY *caresses* PAPO'*s foot.*)

BOBBY: I'm sorry.

(PAPO *pulls his foot away.*)

BOBBY: It's kinda like my birthday.

PAPO: Today?

BOBBY: Yeah.

PAPO: Why didn't you tell me anything? I woulda...

BOBBY: Woulda what?

PAPO: Gotten you something.

BOBBY: You got me tape.

(PAPO *stares at* BOBBY, *who continues his task.* PAPO *gets up and get his brick.*)

PAPO: Happy birthday.

(BOBBY *stares at the brick before taking it.*)

PAPO: I was gonna fucking give it to you anyway. I didn't have a chance to wrap it. It's a paperweight.

(BOBBY *takes the brick. He places it on a pile of pictures he has cut out.*)

BOBBY: It works.

PAPO: You want to call your family or something?

BOBBY: You're my family.

PAPO: You want to go to Blimpie's?

BOBBY: I rather you brought it back home.

PAPO: Okay. (*He puts on his shoes.*) Meatball hero, right?

(BOBBY *nods. He goes back to his task.*)

BOBBY: And a cake.

PAPO: Where am I gonna get a fucking cake?

BOBBY: Okay, a slice of cake.

PAPO: If you ask for candles I'm a smack you.

(PAPO *exits. Returns and kisses* BOBBY *on the top of the head.*)

(*Outside of peep show.* BRIAN *is walking by, very slowly. He sees* PAPO. BRIAN *smiles,* PAPO *smirks and looks away.* BRIAN *starts to walk away.*)

PAPO: What's the matter, man? You don't say hello?

BRIAN: I thought you were mad at me.

PAPO: I should be.

BRIAN: I've been looking for you.

PAPO: You can't have been looking too hard. I'm always right here.

BRIAN: You're not wearing the sweater.

PAPO: Yeah, well, I don't wear it everyday, you know. I gotta give it a rest.

BRIAN: So, how are you doing?

PAPO: Look, are you buying or what?

BRIAN: I just wanted to see you, to talk. I thought you might be happy to see me.

PAPO: Well I ain't.

(BRIAN *looks down at* PAPO's *crotch.*)

BRIAN: I think you are.

PAPO: That's not fair, man. I don't wear underwears.

BRIAN: I just wanted to say I'm sorry about the other day.

PAPO: (*Shrugs*) Fuck it.

(BRIAN *turns to enter peep show.*)

PAPO: Hey, where the fuck are you going? Hot damn. You come all the way down here to apologize and then you go try to pick up somebody else.

BRIAN: Sssh. I thought you were still mad at me.

PAPO: I fucking should be.

BRIAN: Would you like to go to dinner?

PAPO: Time is money.

BRIAN: Can you take some time off?

PAPO: What you think, I punch a fucking time clock?

BRIAN: You got such a mouth on you.

PAPO: Yeah, good lips, huh?

BRIAN: Do I have to pay you to take you to dinner?

PAPO: Hey, don't stand in front of me, you're blocking my fucking view.

(*When* BRIAN *shifts he begins to stare at somebody else.*)

PAPO: You know, it's not like I ain't got other mother fuckers waiting for me. You fucking show up out of nowheres and—

(PAPO *notices* BRIAN *staring at someone else. He slaps the back of his head.*)

PAPO: Hey, mother fucker, you planning on taking the whole fucking deuce to dinner?

BRIAN: No, just you. If you'll come.

PAPO: Like if I'm gonna turn down free food.

BRIAN: Do you want to go home and change?

PAPO: No, do you?

(*Blackout. Lights up on restaurant.* PAPO *and* BRIAN *seated at a small round table. Very nice place—linen tablecloth and napkins. In the background* BOBBY *is softly lit. He sits on the bed, smoking, waiting for* PAPO. *He remains seated throughout the scene.*)

PAPO: Is this how you white people eat every day. (*He touches tablecloth and napkins.*) Look, it's all material.

BRIAN: Lower your voice.

PAPO: (*In a basso profundo*) It's all material.

(BRIAN *laughs.*)

PAPO: Seriously, how much does it cost to eat here?

BRIAN: It's my treat. Don't worry about it.

PAPO: The waiter looked at me like I belonged 'cause I came in with you. Hey, where's my napkin holder? You got one of them glass napkin rings. Where's mine?

BRIAN: Here, you can have mine.

PAPO: No, I'll just take one of the little mother fuckers off another table.

BRIAN: Papo, don't.

PAPO: They ain't in use.

BRIAN: Take mine.

(PAPO *gets up and returns with one.*)

PAPO: Ta-da.

BRIAN: Sssh.

PAPO: Am I embarrassing you, faggot?

(BRIAN *looks away.* PAPO *sits.*)

PAPO: Look man, I'm sorry. Really. I won't call you that again. I swears.

BRIAN: Just tell me what you want from the menu.

PAPO: Now you're mad at me.

BRIAN: No, I'm not.

PAPO: Don't fucking be that way.

BRIAN: (*Sharply*) Can you talk without cursing?

PAPO: When did I fucking curse?

BRIAN: You don't even hear it anymore.

PAPO: I hear what I want to hear. You should try it sometime.

BRIAN: You mean some fucking time.

PAPO: That ain't cursing.

BRIAN: Fuck is a verb, not an adjective.

PAPO: Fool, if anybody knows that I do.

BRIAN: Let's make a deal. Let's see if we can have a nice meal with no cursing.

PAPO: Seriously, man, I don't call that cursing. Cursing is when I'm mad at somebody. Like when I "used" to call you faggot. I used that as a curse.

BRIAN: Could you also try to speak a little softer?

PAPO: Maybe if that guy could hold off on the piano for a bit. (*Calls to piano player*) Hey, man.

BRIAN: Papo. Shut up. Now.

(PAPO *stares at* BRIAN *a second, then smiles.*)

PAPO: You getting all butch on me all of a sudden?

BRIAN: Maybe this wasn't such a good idea.

PAPO: I'll be good. Look, I won't say another word. So, what do you do?

BRIAN: I'm a lawyer.

PAPO: Fucking judge must go crazy when he sees you.

BRIAN: Papo.

PAPO: Right.

BRIAN: I've been in New York a little over a year. Just bought a co-op.

PAPO: Nice, nice.

BRIAN: Pretty much a stay-to-myself type. I'm very discreet. Don't have too many gay friends.

PAPO: I ain't gay.

BRIAN: Okay.

PAPO: I'm not.

BRIAN: Fine.

PAPO: When did you know you were a fag...uh, a queer?

BRIAN: Do you care?

(PAPO *shrugs.*)

BRIAN: I always knew it. Sometimes I feel like I'm going to die if I can't have sex; then other times I think I'll die if I do have it.

PAPO: Man, you is how old and you're still a virgin?

(BRIAN *sees waiter. He elbows* PAPO.)

BRIAN: I'll have the house salad with vinaigrette dressing, onion soup, and duck in raspberry sauce.

PAPO: Me, too.

(*Waiter disappears.* BRIAN *takes a drink of water.*)

PAPO: So when can I pop your cherry?

(BRIAN *chokes on water.*)

PAPO: Hey man, I don't mean right here.

BRIAN: Let's just see if we can make it through this dinner without you giving me a heart attack. Okay?

PAPO: Yeah, okay. I have that effect on people sometimes.

BRIAN: Making them choke?

PAPO: (*Sly smile*) That too.

BRIAN: Uh, do you have any family here?

PAPO: I don't wanna talk about them.

BRIAN: Okay.

PAPO: Do you like talking about your parents?

BRIAN: I said okay.

(*Pause*)

PAPO: What do you talk about when you're with your white friends?

BRIAN: What do you mean?

PAPO: I'm no dummy. Talk English to me and I'll understand you.

BRIAN: I don't think you're stupid.

PAPO: Yeah, well, you fucking better not. Talk to me.

BRIAN: Okay, how old are you?

PAPO: Jesus fucking Christ!

BRIAN: Lower your voice.

PAPO: I'm surprised you got any fucking friends. I'm not as old as I look.

BRIAN: I just wanted to know how long you've been at it.

PAPO: You mean fucking fags?

(BRIAN *tenses.* PAPO *puts his hand on* BRIAN's *arm and mouths "Sorry".*)

BRIAN: This is not working.

PAPO: Sure it is, just fucking relax.

BRIAN: You get angry at everything I say.

PAPO: No I don't. I started at fifteen.

BRIAN: Why?

PAPO: I don't know. I was a real delicacy then. Flavor of the month. The last Coca-Cola in the desert. I made a lot of money.

BRIAN: What's a lot of money?

PAPO: I once made three hundred dollars in one day.

(BRIAN *whistles appreciatively.* PAPO *smiles.*)

BRIAN: That is a lot of money.

PAPO: I gave most of it to my parents. They bought a new living room set.

BRIAN: What did you have to do to earn it?

(PAPO *gives* BRIAN *a dirty look.*)

BRIAN: Sorry.

PAPO: Most people think that all Puerto Ricans are strung-out hustlers. I read, you know. I do fucking crossword puzzles. I don't do drugs. You don't have to be embarrassed by me. I'm not stupid.

BRIAN: I never said you were stupid.

PAPO: You like me, right?

BRIAN: Yeah.

PAPO: Then talk to me. Trust me, I'll understand you.

BRIAN: What do you want me to say?

PAPO: You're a lawyer. Why did you become a lawyer?

BRIAN: To make money.

PAPO: See? We got things in common.

(BRIAN *laughs.*)

BRIAN: I put myself through law school. I almost had to drop out twice.

PAPO: Why?

BRIAN: Money.

PAPO: I thought all white people had money.

BRIAN: We don't. I once had to carry two jobs and keep my grades up.

PAPO: Shit.

BRIAN: Now I've got a good job and I make good money.

PAPO: Yeah?

BRIAN: I'm not rich, but I can buy things for myself now and then. Pamper myself. Take friends to dinner.

(PAPO *smiles.*)

BRIAN: Things I read about but could never afford to do.

(PAPO'*s hand begins to fondle* BRIAN *under the table.*)

BRIAN: Don't do that.

(PAPO *continues.*)

PAPO: (*Teasing*) Why not? You no like?

BRIAN: Please put your hands on top of the table.

PAPO: Lower your voice.

(BRIAN *reaches under the table to remove* PAPO's *hand.*)

PAPO: It looks even worse with both of our hands under here.

(BRIAN *whips his hand out.* PAPO *continues groping.*)

PAPO: This is better.

BRIAN: Please stop.

PAPO: No one can see us. Relax. Drink a little fucking water. You feel real healthy down here.

BRIAN: The waiter is coming.

PAPO: Tell him to go the fuck away.

BRIAN: We're not quite ready yet.

(PAPO *continues groping.*)

BRIAN: Please, this is enough. Stop it.

PAPO: Take me back to your place?

(BRIAN *shakes his head "No".*)

BRIAN: (*Whispers*) Yes.

PAPO: Do you have any fantasy you want to live out?

BRIAN: I just don't want to die.

(PAPO *freezes.*)

PAPO: Do you really want me to stop?

BRIAN: If you stop I'll die.

(*Blackout.* BOBBY *hears a noise in the hallway and hurriedly puts out the cigarette. He opens the window and tries to air the room by waving his hands. He is stopped by the silence in the hallway. He listens by the door. He is about to relight his cigarette again, but stops. He gently drops the cigarette out the window. He waves goodbye to it as it falls. Lights fade out on* BOBBY.)

(*Lights up on* BRIAN, *who is asleep among his sheets.* PAPO *enters. He carries a supermarket bag and places it on the floor. He exits and returns, wheeling a portable T V set, and positions it in front of the bed. He is carrying the remote control for it in his mouth. He exits again and returns with two plates, two spoons, and a knife. He puts the plates on the bed, trying to be as quiet as possible so as not to awaken* BRIAN. PAPO's *mood is very up. He takes a pint of ice cream and a pound cake from the bag. He cuts the cake in half, putting a half on each plate. He opens the ice cream and divides it the same way. He puts the knife aside, puts the ice cream container in the bag, and then quickly, but quietly, strips. He gently gets into bed and puts both plates on his lap. He aims the remote control at the T V. Loud cartoon music is heard.* BRIAN *jumps up.)*

PAPO: Good morning.

BRIAN: What the hell? Lower that goddamn thing!

PAPO: Shit. And you talk about my mother fucking mouth.

BRIAN: What's going on here?

PAPO: I made breakfast in bed. Here.

(PAPO *hands* BRIAN *a plate.)*

PAPO: And they're doing Bugs Bunny. The old ones.

BRIAN: Could you lower that a little?

PAPO: Man, if I put it any lower I won't be able to fucking hear it. (*He lowers the volume.)* You got a real problem with sound, you know that?

(BRIAN *lays back and watches* PAPO, *who is lost in his cartoons.)*

BRIAN: I've got to take a shower.

PAPO: You've had three since we got here. (*He continues eating. He watches the cartoons and reacts to them. He takes* BRIAN's *hand with his free hand.)* You still think God is gonna strike you dead?

BRIAN: What?

(PAPO *laughs at the cartoon.*)

PAPO: What's up doc?

BRIAN: I have to go to work.

(PAPO *tries to kiss him with his mouth full of ice cream.*
BRIAN *turns his head.*)

PAPO: Time for a quickie?

(BRIAN *jumps from the bed and pulls the sheet around him.*)

BRIAN: Do you want to, uh, do you want to take a
shower first?

(PAPO *takes the remote and ups the volume.* BRIAN *takes it
from him and shuts off the T V.* PAPO *studies his ice cream.*)

BRIAN: I don't want to be late.

PAPO: I guess you're done with this spic, huh?

(BRIAN *gets his wallet and places it gently on the bed next to*
PAPO.)

BRIAN: Papo, I am petrified of you. (*He tries to smooth*
PAPO's *head but* PAPO *violently shakes him off.*)

PAPO: So you kicking me out, right? (*Silence*) Are you
kicking me out?

BRIAN: Yes.

(PAPO *puts his plate on the bed and gets dressed. He begins
to put on a shoe.*)

BRIAN: Will you please take some money from me?

(*Without looking up,* PAPO *throws the shoe at* BRIAN.
PAPO *gets himself under control and puts on his other shoe.*
BRIAN *brings the shoe to him and stands by* PAPO *with it
in his hand.* PAPO *takes it and puts it on. He never looks
up at* BRIAN. *When* PAPO *stands he punches* BRIAN *in the
stomach.* BRIAN *doubles over as* PAPO *exits.*)

(*Flophouse.* BOBBY *is sleeping while hugging a pillow.*
PAPO *enters. He stares at* BOBBY *and quietly walks to the
bed where he gently kisses* BOBBY, *who continues sleeping.*
PAPO *goes to the hot plate and takes a sauce pan from it. He
uncovers it and begins to eat Rice-a-roni directly from it. He
sits on the bed, next to* BOBBY, *who slowly wakes up.*)

PAPO: Hey, Baby.

(BOBBY *shimmies up to* PAPO *and lays his head in his lap.*)

PAPO: Got a little lost looking for the cake.

BOBBY: Sssh. How'd it go, Reggie?

PAPO: Not too good, Baby. A lot of distractions. Didn't
get jackshit done. Just ran around with my finger up
my ass.

(BOBBY *giggles.* PAPO *begins to feed him like a baby.
Tenderly, playfully:*)

PAPO: You keeping out of mischief?

BOBBY: Uh-huh.

PAPO: Good boy.

BOBBY: Gimme a kiss, Reggie.

(*A knock is heard.*)

PAPO: (*To door*) Hold on a second.

(PAPO *gives* BOBBY *a kiss.* BOBBY *throws his arms around*
PAPO's *neck.* PAPO *must pull him off.*)

PAPO: Look Baby, that's the man from downstairs and
he wants his rent.

BOBBY: Ronald.

PAPO: Right. Look, I bullshitted the night away and we
has got to pay the rent.

BOBBY: Don't let him in.

(PAPO *kisses* BOBBY *on the shoulder.*)

PAPO: Baby, he's just gonna touch you a little, that's all.

(Another knock is heard. PAPO *yells to door.)*

PAPO: Hey fucking dickhead, fucking chill out for a second. *(He goes to door and opens it. Doorway light comes into room.)* You all fucking ready and set to explode?

*(*PAPO *pulls the sheet off* BOBBY, *who is face down and eating from the pan. A whistle from the man is heard.)*

PAPO: Good, huh?

*(*PAPO *motions for the man to enter and he turns to leave.* BOBBY *reaches out and takes* PAPO's *hand.)*

BOBBY: Okay, but you stay. You stay. You promise.

(The lights from the doorway and the room begin to dim. BOBBY *closes his eyes and squeezes* PAPO's *hand.)*

BOBBY: This is for you.

(Blackout)

PAPO: With one guy I'm an open sore. The one thing I am I can't be with him. I'm good at sex, real good, but I can't do it with him because it makes him nervous. Hey, but wait a second, lemme rewind my past and I'll erase it. I'll be nice and clean for the big white hunter. And I still won't be good enough for him. But I can go to nice places with him, I can go to stores and not have store detectives follow me as if I were gonna steal something. He's one of them and if I'm with him I must be okay, too. White by marriage. Which with Baby would be pretty useless. I mean, to be white and poor I might as well stay the way I fucking am. Then you start falling in love. You know, the stupid stuff. What kind of guy falls in love with another guy? With two other guys? Yeah, 'cause once you start with that shit it takes on a fucking life of its own. My life.

(Night. PAPO *enters phone booth. Lights up on* BRIAN, *in bathrobe, in his bedroom.* BRIAN's *phone rings.)*

PAPO: Hi, Brian, this is Papo.

BRIAN: Ah, listen, I'm about getting ready to leave.

PAPO: Yeah, where to?

BRIAN: I'm meeting some friends for dinner.

PAPO: So you wanna hang out later?

BRIAN: We'll be out late.

PAPO: That's okay.

BRIAN: I don't think so.

PAPO: C'mon man. Fuck, if you're just half as horny as I am we'll set the sheets on fire.

(BRIAN *hangs up.* PAPO *is left holding a dead receiver. He starts to hit the phone with the receiver. He fishes into his pocket for another quarter and calls* BRIAN.)

BRIAN: Papo, please.

PAPO: Don't you ever, ever fucking hang up on me.

(BRIAN *hangs up.* PAPO *inserts another quarter while hitting the phone booth in a rage. He yells at someone waiting to use the phone.*)

PAPO: I ain't fucking finished yet. You wanna do something about it, huh? Wait your goddamn turn, cunt.

(PAPO *flails with one hand at someone waiting for the phone while dialing with the other hand. The phone rings and rings.*)

PAPO: Please pick up.

(BRIAN *finally picks up.*)

BRIAN: Papo.

PAPO: Do you want me to go over there, is that it? Do you want me to show up where you work? I will, you know I will. Don't fuck with me, Brian.

(Pause)

BRIAN: What do you want from me?

PAPO: Why can't I see you?

BRIAN: Papo.

PAPO: I ain't so fucking bad. And you like me, I know you do.

BRIAN: Look, Papo... Okay, I'll meet you at the Peep Show in twenty minutes.

PAPO: I'm right outside your apartment. I'm calling from the corner.

BRIAN: You're what?!

PAPO: Don't get mad, man. I'm just hanging out.

BRIAN: Are you spying on me?

PAPO: No, no, I swear.

BRIAN: Walk away from my building. I'll meet you at Thirty-fourth and Fifth in ten minutes.

PAPO: Yeah, okay.

BRIAN: If I see you at the phone booth when I leave the building I'll turn around and go right back in.

PAPO: And I'll fucking crack your head in. *(Pause)* Thirty-fourth and Fifth.

BRIAN: Thirty-fourth and Fifth.

PAPO: Well, fucking hurry up.

(BRIAN hangs up.)

PAPO: `Cause I miss you.

(Thirty-fourth and Fifth. PAPO is wearing BRIAN's sweater. Enter BRIAN.)

PAPO: Yo man, fancy meeting you here.

BRIAN: Hi, Papo.

PAPO: Check out the sweater, man. I'm wearing the sweater you bought for me.

BRIAN: What do you want?

PAPO: Hey, just a little action. That's all.

(*He playfully grabs* BRIAN *who moves away.*)

BRIAN: Are you crazy? This is not the Peep Show.

PAPO: Oh yeah, I forgot. Decent people hang out here.

BRIAN: That's not it.

PAPO: People who never have sex.

BRIAN: Look, I've got to get up early tomorrow.

PAPO: So what? You were gonna meet your white friends for dinner, weren't you?

BRIAN: They're friends, period. And I called and canceled.

PAPO: Shit. You weren't gonna meet nobody. You were probably at home playing with your meat when I called.

(BRIAN *starts to walk away,* PAPO *follows.*)

PAPO: Let's go back to your place.

BRIAN: I don't ever want you in my home again.

PAPO: And have a little party. Take one of the side streets, there are less people there.

(*On a dimmer street.* PAPO *grabs* BRIAN *and kisses him.*)

BRIAN: This has got to stop.

PAPO: Okay.

BRIAN: I mean it. Don't call me, don't follow me.

PAPO: Fine. Don't desire me.

BRIAN: Your ego, like your brain, is in your crotch.

PAPO: No man, I don't think so.

BRIAN: You don't think, period.

PAPO: `Cause I ain't the only one doing the following.

BRIAN: You're crazy.

PAPO: And I ain't the one who checked out the meat the first chance I got.

(BRIAN *turns to leave;* PAPO *grabs his arm.*)

PAPO: I get my rocks off seven times a day. How do you do?

(PAPO *slowly pulls* BRIAN *toward him.*)

PAPO: I don't think you do too well. I think you probably got a real tired hand.

BRIAN: I can't. Please. I just want to go back to the way it was—

PAPO: The only trouble with being alone is there's no one there to kiss back.

BRIAN: —before I met you.

(PAPO *holds* BRIAN *and kisses him.*)

PAPO: Now you kiss me.

BRIAN: I can't.

PAPO: I'm not gonna fucking move. You kiss me.

(BRIAN *and* PAPO *stare at each other.* BRIAN *slowly moves toward* PAPO.)

PAPO: Keep your eyes open. I want you to see who you're kissing.

(BRIAN *kisses* PAPO. *The kiss builds in passion until* PAPO *breaks free.*)

PAPO: No, you don't wanna see me. Tell me you don't wanna see me.

BRIAN: (*In a small voice*) I don't want to see you.

PAPO: You know, you're really full of shit, man. You'd rather be home jerking off by yourself. Is that it?

BRIAN: No.

(PAPO *kisses* BRIAN.)

PAPO: Is that it?

BRIAN: (*Whispers*) No.

PAPO: No what?

BRIAN: Don't go.

PAPO: Why not?

BRIAN: Please.

PAPO: Are you horny? (*Silence*) Let me hear you say it, man. Are you horny?

BRIAN: I'm horny.

(PAPO *puts his arms around* BRIAN.)

PAPO: What do you want me to do about it? Put your arms around my neck.

BRIAN: We're in the middle of the street.

PAPO: It's dark, man.

(BRIAN *does*.)

PAPO: Maybe I can help you do what you do alone.

BRIAN: Yes, please.

PAPO: But where? You told me you don't want me in your home. I'm too dirty for your home, right?

(PAPO *kisses* BRIAN *as they embrace. A car goes by; someone yells "Faggot".* BRIAN *tries to break free.* PAPO *holds him.* BRIAN *stops struggling and they kiss again.*)

PAPO: I'll see you around, Brian. (*He begins to walk away.*) Have to go back to where I belong. Got a nice, seventeen-year-old white boy waiting up for me. You better hurry home, too. You don't want to keep your hand waiting.

(BRIAN *follows* PAPO *and begins to hit him.* PAPO *tries to hold his hands and they begin to fight.* PAPO *wraps his arms around* BRIAN, *pinning his arms down.*)

PAPO: Say it.

BRIAN: Fuck you.

PAPO: Say it or I walk.

(*Pause*)

BRIAN: Please come home with me.

(PAPO *lets* BRIAN *go.*)

PAPO: Why?

BRIAN: `Cause I want you.

PAPO: How much do you want me?

BRIAN: I want you.

PAPO: I don't believe you.

BRIAN: I want you.

PAPO: I still don't believe you.

(BRIAN *gets on his knees.*)

BRIAN: I want you.

(PAPO *kneels with* BRIAN. *They embrace.*)

(*Blackout*)

(*Flophouse*)

BOBBY: Please don't go, please don't go, please don't go.

PAPO: This is my last chance. I ain't no sweet-looking little kid anymore. I've got mileage on me and it's beginning to show.

BOBBY: You got somebody else.

PAPO: Yeah.

BOBBY: I love you, Reggie.

PAPO: Well, he loves me too. And he knows my name.

BOBBY: Do you like him better than you like me?

PAPO: I must.

BOBBY: He's never gonna love you like I love you.

PAPO: I didn't have to come back here to tell you, you know. What the hell do I have here that I have to take with me?

BOBBY: You mean besides my heart?

(PAPO *hits* BOBBY.)

BOBBY: I don't want to fight with you, Reggie.

PAPO: C'mon Shithead. You fucking pissed off, right? Go ahead, hit me. Hit me.

(PAPO *continues to jab at* BOBBY, *who grabs* PAPO's *hand and kisses it.*)

BOBBY: I love you.

(PAPO *pushes* BOBBY *away.*)

PAPO: Cut the fucking shit. You love Reggie, not me. What the fuck am I supposed to do, turn tricks until we're old and gray?

BOBBY: I'm yours, Papo. I'm your Baby.

PAPO: I never asked for you, you fucking fruitcake.

(BOBBY *reaches between the mattress and box spring and pulls out his knife. He tries to stab himself.* PAPO *wrests the knife from him. He sits on the floor, cradling* BOBBY.)

BOBBY: Oh please don't go. Please.

PAPO: Sssh, sssh. Ronald's a good guy. He loves you too, Baby.

BOBBY: You're the one for me.

PAPO: No, I'm the one for me, period. (*He gets up, takes the knife, and heads to the door.*) You'll be okay, guy. You're probably right. Nobody's gonna love me like you do. Even if you don't know who I am.

BOBBY: I don't know who you are? I don't know who you fucking are?! I can be you, anybody can be you. What's so fucking tough about pushing people away? But can you be me? Come on, Papo, can you be me? Can you love anybody the way I love you? I know who you are. I love you.

PAPO: Get the fuck outta my face.

BOBBY: I know who you are. I love you, Papo.

PAPO: And you call me by somebody else's name?

BOBBY: Would it have made any difference if I called you Papo?

(PAPO *exits.*)

BOBBY: When did I stop being your Baby?

(BOBBY *goes to window. Lights dim as he opens it.*)

(*Lights up on street.* PAPO *enters and begins to walk. A siren approaches and crowd voices are heard.*)

VOICE 1: What happened?

VOICE 2: Some little white boy in panties jumped out the window.

VOICE 1: I think he's dead.

VOICE 3: One less faggot.

(PAPO *pauses, staring straight ahead. After a few beats he continues walking, totally expressionless. He slowly begins to shake. He runs toward the flophouse and cradles* BOBBY'*s body.*)

PAPO: It'll be okay, Baby. You're my baby and I'm here. I'm right here.

(The music from the beginning of the play starts, with the voices and the sirens. PAPO rocks BOBBY's body. He removes sweater [the one BRIAN gave him] and wraps it around BOBBY. He continues to rock him as the music, voices, and lights begin to dim.)

PAPO: Bring back my heart, you little mother fucker.

END OF PLAY